THE FUGITIVE SLAVE LAW:

A SERMON,

PREACHED IN THE

Fourth Congregational Church,

Norwich, Conn., June 25th, 1854.

BY REV. CHARLES P. BUSH,

PASTOR.

PUBLISHED BY REQUEST.

NORWICH:

WOODWORTH & PERRY, STEAM PRINTERS, FRANKLIN SQUARE.

1854.

The following Discourse was prepared and preached to my people, without reference to publication. A number of my parishioners have, however, expressed a desire to possess it in a more permanent form, and have it more widely circulated. After making a few verbal alterations, I have, therefore given it to the press, by their direction and request, with the hope that it may contribute, in some humble measure, to swell the increasing tide of opposition to legalized kidnapping.

C. P. B.

GREENEVILLE, NORWICH, July, 1854.

DISCOURSE.

DUTERONOMY XXIII. 15, 16. THOU SHALT NOT DELIVER UNTO HIS MASTER, THE SERVANT WHICH IS ESCAPED FROM HIS MASTER UNTO THEE; HE SHALL DWELL WITH THEE, EVEN AMONG YOU IN THAT PLACE WHICH HE SHALL CHOOSE IN ONE OF THY GATES, WHERE IT LIKETH HIM BEST: THOU SHALT NOT OPPRESS HIM.

We have no right to do wrong. This *was* a truism. But there is a law of our land which seems to make it a mooted question. We refer to that which requires the rendition of fugitives from Southern bondage. This law was passed four years ago. We then gave our views of its inhumanity, in a Thanksgiving sermon. But recent events have brought the subject up again and given it a painful, and even appalling prominence. The whole land is stirred, as by a moral earthquake. The pulpit and the press are teeming with the subject. And well they may be; for this is a subject of the greatest possible importance. It is a great *moral* question. There is a right and a wrong about it; we ought to inquire after the right. It is a question upon which *God* has spoken. We ought to seek after His will. It is intimately connected with the spread of Christ's kingdom. Our hands are enfeebled because they are stained with blood. Our missionaries have often felt this, whilst trying to commend the religion of America to the heathen. They have been among the first to come to the light on the whole subject of slavery, for they have felt that even the heathen would see how irreconcilable it is with the religion of the gospel.

And then this Fugitive Slave Law intimately affects the welfare of more than three million of our fellow-men now held in cruel bondage in this "land of the free." It is one of the strong links in the chain that binds them. Indeed, it affects the *whole South.* It is the testimony of thousands of the most competent Southerners themselves, that slavery is demoralizing in its influence on the whole of society; and the Fugitive Slave Law is designed to aid in upholding the whole system, with all its demoralizing tendencies.

This law is also one of a series of determined and desperate measures for extending and perpetuating this awful system of American Slavery, until the whole land shall be brought under its corrupting influences.

Let me add, this Fugitive Slave Law is, and must be, offensive in the sight of God. It is one of those gigantic, national sins, for which every reflecting christian must feel that we have reason to fear Divine judgments.

Surely, I need say no more to show how important the subject is, or how much it deserves our attention, even aside from the recent painful, humiliating events which give it a peculiar importance. When these are added, necessity is laid upon us. It is time something more were said, and much more done, if possible, to arrest the spreading power of this monstrous wickedness.

We believe this is now very generally felt. But as to what should be said, and what should be done, minds will honestly differ. And it is a subject upon which difference of opinion is apt to be attended with excitement. It is a painful subject, and can hardly be considered without excitement. Not to *feel* on such a subject is inhuman. And yet wisely to regulate our feelings, and kindly to temper our speech, is not only a christian duty, but best promotes also the end at which we aim. Over-excitement and intemperate speech injure any cause. We design therefore to speak calmly but firmly, plainly but kindly, leaving each one to judge for himself, in the fear of God, as to the truth of what we say.

The great truth or duty which we wish to assert at the present time, is well presented in the very language of the text, which I will repeat: "Thou shalt not deliver unto his master the servant that is escaped from his master unto thee; he shall dwell with thee, even among you in that place which he shall choose in one of thy gates, where it liketh him best: thou shalt not oppress him." Or, in other words, *we have no right to deliver up the fugitive. The law which requires it is wrong in morals, and cannot be binding on us.*

This is our position. We prefer thus plainly, distinctly, to state it at the outset, for we think it can be justified.

I. To deliver up the fugitive is to make war on his ***in-alienable rights.*** He has rights which God gave him, over and above all human laws. This was a self-evident truth in 1776. It is no less a truth now, although some seem to forget it.

I meet a fellow man in the street*; his face is darker than mine; he is on his way to Canada: have I any right to stop him? Have I any right to seize and bind him, and send him back to Virginia? If I were ten times as strong as I am now, would that confer upon me any right? If I were as strong as the United States Government, would that confer upon me any such right? How plain is the answer to these questions. *Might* does not make *right.* And yet this is all the right there is in the Fugitive Slave Law. It is the strong forcibly wresting from the weak his *inalienable rights;* tearing

*Here and in one or two other places I use the same argument, in nearly the same words, of a brief article I recently furnished for the Examiner. I use the same, for it best expresses my ideas on the point.

from our poor brother, simply because we have the power, that which God gave him as exclusively his own.

Certainly, that about "*inalienable rights*," which found its way into our Declaration of Independence, was not a mere rhetorical flourish. If it was, our revolution was an unjustifiable *rebellion*, and we ought to return to our allegiance to Great Britain as soon as possible. But if it was not, then this poor fugitive has these rights. He has never forfeited them. He has just as good a right to "life, liberty and the pursuit of happiness," as any other person in all the land. He has just as good a right to choose, for himself and family, his place of abode, his occupation, as any other man, high or low, black or white. If he chooses to go to Canada, I have no more right to stop him than I have to stop President Pierce or Lord Elgin, on the same journey. All the inhabitants of this town have no more. All the inhabitants of the United States have no more. He has broken no law, human or divine, in running away. He has only done that which God gave him a perfect right to do. And as such a person stands before me now, in the actual *possession* of these inalienable rights, it is just as wicked for me to reduce him again to bondage, as it would be for me to go to the coast of Africa, and seize a man there, and reduce him to bondage. The Government has no more right to kidnap a man in a free State than they have on the coast of Africa; no more right to enslave a colored man than they have a white; no more right to march off Anthony Burns, amidst bristling bayonets and at the cannon's mouth, than they have to serve Governor Washburn, or Mayor Smith of Boston, in the same way. And surely, the mere fact that a poor man has *once* been deprived of his inalienable rights, is no reason why he should be again. Or the fact that the Government is stronger than an individual, is no reason why the Government should do wrong any more than an individual.

If indeed there be any such thing as "inalienable rights," then these are simple self-evident truths. We have endeavored to state them in the simplest possible language, that their truthfulness might be the more manifest. And it does seem as though there was no denying any one of them.

And if so, then the conclusion is inevitable that the Fugitive Slave Law is at war with the inalienable rights of the poor fugitive.

II. And if this be so, it is also against the law of God, for God requires us to respect the rights of our fellow man. Yea, it is against the express statutes of the Divine law. The text is clear and conclusive. Whether it respects slaves, escaping from surrounding nations and coming amongst the Israelites, or servants of the Hebrews fleeing from their masters, it makes no difference; they were to be unmolested; they might choose their own dwelling-place. God here recognizes these inalienable rights to life, liberty and the pursuit of happiness.

But even though we entirely mistake in the interpretation of this passage, the "golden rule," "All things, therefore, whatsoever ye would that men should do to you, do ye even so to them," makes our duty plain. If *we* were fleeing from oppression, should we like to have one stronger than we, seize us, and bind us, and carry us back to unrequited toil? We have no more right to seize another. Indeed, the act is just as plainly a violation of moral and divine law as stealing or murder. And when we come to look at this thing just as it is, it is plain that we have no more right to execute this Fugitive Slave Law than we have to murder or to steal; the Government has none. In fact, if, as so many patriot orators have told us, liberty is worth more than life, it is *worse* to reduce a man to bondage than it is to take his life. For one, I would no sooner lift a finger to help execute the Fugitive

Slave Law, than I would lift the. assassin's dagger and plunge it into the heart of a fellow man and deprive him of life. Before God, I have no more right to do the one than I have to do the other.

III. This Fugitive Slave Law is *at war* with the Constitution of the United States. We are not an assemblage of lawyers, or judges, or the Supreme Court of the United States, nevertheless we have just as good a right to our opinion on this subject as the Supreme Court itself. And there are some things about the subject so plain that he "may read that runs." It requires no peculiar sagacity to see that there are irreconcilable discrepancies between this Fugitive Slave Act and some of the fundamental principles, and some of the chief provisions and safeguards of our glorious Constitution.

The Constitution was adopted, as it is said in the preamble, to "establish justice, insure domestic tranquility, provide for the common defense, promote the general welfare and secure the blessings of liberty to ourselves and our posterity." This Fugitive Slave Law is at war with all these glorious ends.

The Constitution says that no person shall be "deprived of life, *liberty*, or property, without due process of law." This law is executed with a very *un*due process.

The Constitution provides that "in all criminal prosecutions" there shall be a trial by "an impartial jury." The fugitive is *treated* as a criminal; and yet he has no trial by jury.

The Constitution provides that a crimimal shall "be confronted with the witnesses against him," face to face, and have the privilege of cross-questioning them. In this case, a mere certificate of a magistrate, taken in a distant State, no matter with what bias, or with what intent to defraud, shall be taken as final and conclusive, even against the liberty of a fellow man and of his posterity to the end of time.

Or again, "In suits at common law," the Constitution provides, that "where the value in controversy exceeds twenty dollars, the right of trial by jury shall be preserved." Surely, a man is worth more than twenty dollars to himself; and yet where he is himself in controversy the right of trial by jury is denied him.

It is thus that the law is at war with some of the plainest principles of the Constitution, as well as many of the dearest rights of man, which that truly venerable and excellent instrument professes sacredly to guard. Accordingly, many of the ablest men in the country, both North and South, regard the law as unconstitutional. And if words mean any thing, it was held, even by Daniel Webster, in his real judgment, that that clause in the Constitution which provides for the rendition of fugitives did not contemplate such a law at all; that it conferred upon Congress no power to make such a law. He says, "I have always thought that the Constitution addressed itself to the legislatures of the States themselves. * * * * * It is said that a person escaping into another State, and becoming therefore within the jurisdiction of that State, shall be delivered up. It seems to me that the plain import of the passage is, that the State itself, in obedience to the injunction of the Constitution, shall cause him to be delivered up. This is my judgment. I have always entertained it; I entertain it now." Mr. Rhett, a Senator from South Carolina, in 1850, warmly advocated the same sentiment. Robert Rantoul, of Mass., the same. A Judge in Wisconsin has recently discharged a fugitive on the ground that the law is unconstitutional, for this as well as other reasons.*

And beside all these Constitutional objections, there are some other features of this law so unjust and so odious that

*The *Supreme Court* of Wisconsin has since confirmed the decision of the Judge above alluded to, and a Commissioner in Columbus, Ohio, has resigned his office on the ground that the law is unconstitutional.

all our moral nature revolts at the barbarity. It is especially provided that its process shall be "*summary.*" There is an indecent haste about it. It would not subject the slave-holder to the least inconvenience of delay in reclaiming his property. It thinks more of a slight inconvenience or expense on his part than it does of life and liberty to another, who is claimed as a slave. A poor fellow was thus hurried off from New York, without even time to let his wife and children know what had befallen him. Whilst they looked for his return at night, he was already on his way South to wear out the remnant of his days for another.

This law places too much power also in the hands of a single man, and he but a subordinate, *petty* officer of Government. And yet this *inferior* officer, not even a judge—a mere commissioner—constitutes the entire court; judge, jury, arbitrator and all. And his decision is final and unquestionable. There is no review, no appeal. We have already seen that the Constitution does not allow twenty dollars' worth of goods in litigation to be so imperiled. And why should the liberty of a man be?

But worse than all else, the law offers a distinct, direct *bribe* for a decision adverse to the interests of the poor fugitive—giving the Commissioner ten dollars if he decides that the person on trial is a slave, only five dollars if he is obliged to decide that he is a freeman! Was there ever any thing more monstrous in human legislation? Was a court ever constituted with more express reference to making it corrupt and false in all it does? We have never seen any apology offered for this anomaly in the law. We think it well that none has been attempted, for it is incapable of explanation. It bears on its face unmistakable evidence of its base intent.

Of course, a law so open to abuse, will *be* abused,—has *been* abused. Those who were truly free must have been dragged away to hopeless captivity. In the very first case tried under this law, a free man* was carried off to Maryland. The Marshal believed he was free, and would not leave him at the State line, as he might have done, but followed him even to the door of the supposed master, and there the mistake was acknowledged and the man was returned. Another in Indiana was thus taken, the claimant himself being present, and the proof being satisfactory to the Commissioner. But all was false, and the man recovered two thousand dollars damages for being thus kidnapped. In another case a whole family of free persons, living quietly in their home in Indiana, were seized and marched off by a gang of ruffian claimants. The citizens knowing they were free, turned out in a body and brought them back.

These are some of the mistakes which have been *discovered.* How many more have occurred which have not been discovered, we know not. But can that law be just which thus imperils the liberties of freemen?

But still it may be said that we have *agreed* to deliver up the fugitive—there is such a provision in the Constitution. We grant that there is such a clause, so understood by some. But if we had that document to make over again, the free States would not now consent to such a provision. Our fathers would not have consented to it, except as they supposed that slavery would soon die out, and their consent could do but little harm. No! Although when that Constitution was made there was but one free State and twelve slave States, yet our patriot fathers really meant to make that instrument as favorable as possible to freedom. There is abundant historic evidence of this fact, and that they anticipated for the whole land a speedy riddance from this terrible evil; and they intended that the bond of our Union should be such as is proper for a people entirely, nobly free.

But even on the supposition that we have agreed to return

*Gibson, of Philadelphia.

the fugitive, that does not make it right. If we had agreed a thousand times to do wrong, that does not make it right. Judas *agreed* to betray his Master; that did not make it right. Forty men once bound themselves under an oath that they would neither eat nor drink till they had killed Paul; that did not make murder right. The crew of a pirate-ship generally have written *articles* of agreement—a "constitution;" and they generally bind themselves by the strongest oaths that it is possible for men to utter, to stand by each other in blood and crime; but that doos not make piracy a virtue.

But now, it may be asked, what shall we do? I answer, First, violence can do no good. It is not a case which calls for *revolution*, therefore, *armed resistance* to law is itself a moral wrong. We cannot overthrow the Government if we would, and we *would* not if we could. Corrupt as we believe so many of our public acts and public men to be, still our Government is the best in the world. We do not wish to change it for any other. And the Government is solemnly bound to maintain itself against all rebellion and all treason. *The officers of Government* are bound to execute this law—*or resign their office.* They have a right to do the latter. If they believe, as we do, that the law is wrong, they ought to do the latter. And we hope the day will come, when a man can not be found in a free State who will hold office under Government, if it requires him to perform this dreadful work. The people are already prepared highly to honor such as take this noble stand. It *was* taken the other day by a captain of police and watch in Boston. He has become a moral celebrity by so simple and just an act.

But if any will still be officers of the United States Government, they are bound to see the laws of the Government executed. It is periling every interest of society to resist them by armed force, and it can do our cause no manner of good. Yes, even State or City authorities are bound to quell insurrection and riot, springing from any cause whatever. But as the United States Government has transcended its powers, and taken the honorable business of chasing fugitives into its own hands, contrary to the intent of the Constitution, we think it but fair to leave the General Government to do its own chosen work. State and City governments need not *volunteer* their aid, unless they love the employment.

But some will still say, "*We have sworn to support the Constitution.*" Does this mean that the Constitution is *infallible*, and we must not dissent from one of its principles or provisions? That Constitution sanctioned the slave-trade twenty years, and then our Government declared it piracy. Was it any less piracy during those twenty years? Was man-stealing a virtue during that time, and none but saints engaged in it? Or, will any pretend that all the *laws* made by our Government are morally right? Have not our laws robbed the Indian? Have we not directly violated, time and again, the most solemn treaties made with him? Have we not ruthlessly torn him from his home, from his council-fires, from the graves of his ancestors, and driven him, at the point of the bayonet into the wilderness? Are we obliged to approve of *these* laws, and *these* acts, because we have sworn to support the Constitution?

But what then, it may be asked, do you do with the "freeman's oath?" I answer—that oath does not bind me to sustain all the laws that it is possible for a corrupt majority in Congress to pass. If I take that oath at all, I must take it with this reservation:—I will support that constitution and the laws of the land, *so far as they agree with God's law.* I cannot go one hair's breadth further, and yet appeal to God for the sincerity of my heart. We "swear by the greater," or else an oath is good for nothing. God is above all Constitutions, and to be obeyed before all, or there is no propriety in swearing by Him, and our oaths are a mockery.

But still it may be asked, can a *conscientious* man take the freeman's oath, knowing at the same time that there is such a law of the land, which he cannot approve, and the mandates of which, under certain circumstances, he might feel compelled openly to disobey? I answer—with our views, we could not conscientiously be a *Commissioner* or a *Marshal;* but we can be a *citizen.* We can take the oath engaging to support the Constitution and the laws *as a whole;* for in most things they are right. And we cannot do better than this in any land. No government is perfect. If we would to be citizens any where, we must take the oath. But all who really believe that God is greater than human governments, and that human governments are not infallible, must make this reservation, either expressed, or understood. And government has nothing to fear from those who have *such* scruples, but much to fear from those who make no moral distinctions.

"But who shall decide?" it is triumphantly asked, "whether a law is according to God's law or not?" Of course the Government will decide for itself what course it must pursue. And then it is equally clear that each individual must judge for himself. We have no Popes here, in Church or State. The right of private judgment is as dear and sacred in State as in Church; dear as life itself, in either. And whatever way we judge, we must bear the consequences. Government must still go forward with its duties. But Government cannot deny to us the right to suffer, if suffer we must, for our conscientious scruples. The right of *passive resistance* to unjust laws, or those which are honestly regarded as unjust, is as inalienable as any other right.

But that which many regard as a very grave question still remains. Can we thus repudiate our bargain with the South? Having engaged to surrender fugitives may we now refuse? We have put our hand to the plough, and we will not look back—we answer, certainly we may, *in the right way.* If we have agreed to do that which is in itself wrong, nothing is plainer than that still we ought not to do it. And if we ought not to do it, we ought honestly to say we cannot do it, and retract the engagement; giving as our just and only reason, it *is* wrong; we have no right to do it. If half of the crew of a pirate-ship come to their senses and see that they are doing the work of devils, what other course should they pursue except kindly, but firmly to tell their companions that they can go no further? If two men have engaged together to steal a horse, and one of them relents, and asks us what he shall do, should we tell him, "Sir, you must help steal the horse, for you have *agreed* to?" This may be a "doctrine of devils," but it is not the doctrine of the bible, or of good morals, or of good citizenship. And how much is a man better than a horse!

As to the *manner* in which we should revoke our unholy contract to return fugitives, if indeed that is an obligation imposed by the Constitution, I would have it done with all possible kindness toward our Southern brethren. I would reason the case; I would expostulate; I would entreat; I would seek, if possible, an amicable adjustment of our difficulties: but only on this one holy basis—we can have nothing more to do with upholding the dreadful system of slavery, either directly or indirectly. We wash our hands of it. If you *will have slavery*, you must have it to yourselves. If you will reduce those again to bondage who have taken into their own possession that which God gave them, as an inalienable right, you must do it without our aid.

Our first duty therefore is, properly to seek the repeal of the Fugitive Slave Law; in fact, to *demand* its repeal. If we have no right to pass such a law, it ought to be repealed. We have a right to demand it. And recent events have shown that nothing of the kind is too sacred to be repealed.

And then let all the free States, and all the free men, who are willing that this should really be a free country, plant themselves on this one new platform.—No more Slave Territory, no more Slave States ; no Slave Trade between the States, and a *Free Capital* for our glorious Republic. We hope the day has at length come when the great body of Northern freemen are prepared to unite on this grand basis. The poor fugitive demands this union of us. The three millions of bondmen, to whose emancipation this would be a mighty entering wedge, demand it of us. The peace and prosperity of our country demand it. If we *love* those three millions of men, in bonds and darkness, it seems as though we might do this for them. If we love our country, if we remember that corruption brings decay, or that sin provokes divine judgments, it seems as though we might do this. And we honestly believe that in such a movement, we should have the sympathy and prayers of many also at the South. We believe that the number of those is rapidly increasing throughout the land, and all the more for the apparent triumph of corruption and sin in some recent events, who are ready to inscribe upon their banner, "No North, no South, no East, no West; but God, Liberty, and our Country's true welfare." This is the *true* "Union, for the sake of the Union;" this a union upon which the smile of heaven can rest; and there is no safety in union or disunion without that.

Let this policy be carried out in our State Legislatures, in our State laws, in all our municipal corporations. By State resolutions, by State laws, by political action and church action, let us kindly but effectually put an end to all copartnership in this dreadful wickedness.

But would not this lead to disunion and civil war? We think not. If we do right, the God of heaven will defend us. If we continue in the wrong, we cannot say as much.

Or, even if separation should follow, and we should have

two republics instead of one, we think it infinitely preferable to the present state of things. We can not have a true union while slavery is the dominant element in our political organization.

These are some of the things we desired to say at the present time. Much more might be said; much more we should be glad to say, especially in regard to our specific duties in the matter, and the glorious hope we have that a brighter day is dawning upon us. We do not believe that things are to remain as they are. We do not believe that we are to go much lower down in the way of political degradation and ruin. The tide of moral health on this subject is returning. The spirit of Jefferson, and Hancock, and Samuel Adams is rekindled in many a breast. Another revolution, in comparison with which the former shall be hardly mentioned, is at hand. The land will be purged; all will be free; God shall be glorified. To Him we look; and on his goodness, his wisdom and his power we rely, to help in the glorious work of making this truly a free country and a christian people.

www.ingramcontent.com/pod-product-compliance
Lightning Source LLC
LaVergne TN
LVHW020638110826
845149LV00004B/1258
9781418190705